FAITH YOU

~~FAKE~~ IT ~~TIL~~ WILL MAKE IT!

Shalamar Jones

Dedication

I write from a heart full of love for my loving daughter, Nickera, who has made my life a special joy. Thank you for sticking with me through this journey.

My mom, Patricia, lifts me in prayer when I'm low, loves me when I'm unlovable, and makes me believe I am the woman others think I am.

To my friend Kaydeon Stewart-Pierre, who "knows me and likes me anyways, encourages me with her trust, accepts me through her actions, and keeps my feet on a firm foundation.

A God whose presence is personal, whose care is absolute, whose promise is dependable, and whose love is unexplainable.

My guide post, the Holy Spirit, guides and steers me throughout this writing process causing healing wonders to take place in areas of my life that I deemed 'unhealable.'

Successfully Yours,
Shalamar Jones

Contents

Introduction

Today is a beautiful, bountiful, blissful day because every day that God gives us breaths is a glorious day.

I've lived through the vale of depression, from a place where I acknowledged I was joy-immune, and I've walked this journey with chronic pain. Nonetheless, God continues to battle for me every day of this journey. Each day He gives me breath in my lungs, and a song of praise in my soul is a gift to be used for His glory.

While hardships and misfortunes rarely feel like a blessing, especially when we are stuck in the mire and the pain, I've discovered that life's greatest plights are perfect setups for God to do the impossible and prove His faithfulness. He has never broken a promise yet, and it's because of His consistent track record that we can believe in a good day despite our emotions and grueling circumstances.

Today I speak from a place of triumph where I can enjoy all the simple joys God provides to delight my heart. When we focus on God and intentionally look for the simple joys and pleasures around us, our heart grows lighter in gratitude. Whether it's the joy of a new relationship, friendship, autumn flowers, or the whiff of a steaming cup of coffee, God gives us these simple joys to delight and teach us about Him.

There were many years when I was buried in immeasurable tears only to reap his joy now, not because life is uncomplicated or hardships no longer arise, but because I have faith in God. I've come to depend on God's consistency even when I can't see His hand moving. Since God doesn't play favorites, I know that what God is doing for me, He will do for you.

God's devotion, Word, and assurances are offered to all. The Holy Spirit reminds us of all truth and never forces Himself on us. We must acknowledge, accept, and rely on Him and all He has promised.

> ***Father, you are a fair and compassionate God. Only you would think to offer the blessing of joy in exchange for the despair of our tears. Thank you for not distracting us with our tears but instead deeming them so beneficial that you would keep them. What the adversary intends for evil, in your loving kindness, you use for our good and your glory. Help us to keep our eyes on you, for therein is the fullness of joy. In Jesus's name, Amen.***

"The climax of God's happiness is the delight He takes in the echoes of His excellence in the praises of His people."

John Piper

A Posture of Praise

Thank you, Lord, for Your fantastic gift of salvation, which covers my past, present, and future iniquities! It is such an underserved and truly exquisite gift of grace. Let me not take Your blessing lightly, but fill me with the courage to share it with those around me. In Jesus' name, Amen.

Let's be honest: How much time did you spend honoring Jesus today?

Requesting items doesn't count. Reading a passage of scripture doesn't matter, either. I'm inquiring. How much time did you spend making Him know how wonderful, incredible, extraordinary, magnificent, and remarkable He is?

Did you know that we were God's adversary, fated to face His fury? Sit with that for a minute.

Jesus was tormented, persecuted, victimized, oppressed, and tortured on the cross to alleviate the fury of God. Do those facts move you?

Because of the cross, we live as God's children. How can we go a day without praising Him for this goodness?

God lives in us! Yes, nod in awe at this!

Stop reading for a bit and worship Him. Magnify His Holy name. God gives us breath so we can breathe. Use your next breath for its intended purpose. Bless Him.

"Bless the LORD, O my soul, and all that is within me; bless His Holy name!" --Psalm 103:1 is my victory verse. Coincidentally it is one of my favorite songs as well.

We should not start our days without praising the triune God. We are commanded to delight in Him always. Today, nothing you have to do is more meaningful and significant than honoring Him.

If I'm not smart enough to start my day honoring God, why should anyone be attentive to what I have to convey? If I am ridiculous sufficient to refrain from praise because my mind is fixated on problems at work or within my family, then I'm more of a problem than I realize.

Our dearth of praise may be the primary cause of our divisions. Once we eliminate worshiping, all hope for unity, harmony, and agreement is lost. This is what unites us: we can't stop speaking about the glory we find in Jesus.

What if you do not feel like going any further in this book? Take this nugget with you. It's hard to consistently start a dispute with someone who is 'posture in praise'—someone who is ever before God crying out to Him. I have learned in my adult life that many of our problems could be reconciled if we discussed our concerns on our knees before a Holy God. We can't allow the enemy or our enemies to interrupt our posture of praise.

Our posture of praise is our path to unity.

Even now, I encourage you to look up the following passages that explain the abovementioned truths: Romans 5:10-11; Ephesians 2:3-4; Romans 3:23-25; 1 John 3:1; 2 Corinthians 5:21; John 14:21-23.

"Never be afraid to trust an unknown future to a known God."

Corrie Ten Boom

Leaving the Results to God...

God, sometimes I want a fast solution to my issues. It can be challenging to wait, but I know Your timing, will, and plans for my life are flawless. As I wait on you, Lord, help me to understand the current situation I'm in, to focus on the blessings I currently have, and glorify You, Lord, for all the things You're going to do. In Jesus' name, Amen.

There was a time when depression had its grasp so tightly around my chest that even taking my next breath was exhausting due to the overwhelmingness of life.

Have you ever been there before, that dark, lonely place where the pain feels agonizing and your sanity is replenished with chaos and queries?

Was it a call from the physician with information that will change your life as you know it?

A broken relationship or friendship?

The loss of a child or a loved one?

Did you fall short of those who trust you, and now you carry the shame daily?

Perhaps you're currently striding in a season like this and racing to find some serenity amidst the storm. I've been there, and in some ways, still there. I'm not about to promise you instantaneous explanations for your troubles. I am here to notify you that you are not isolated. We have a God who "is near to the broken-hearted and saves those who are crushed in spirit." (Psalm 34:18) and vows that even in the darkest valley, He will be right by our side to reassure and lead the way... (Psalm 23)

Devastating periods of your life are often followed by great moments of victory. We fight not against flesh and blood but against spiritual wickedness in high places. Our battle is spiritual, but we often fail to reckon with the physical factors that affect our struggles.

We must recognize our greatest weapons against dark periods of our lives. We should study the word, memorize it, and do it. Pray regularly and thoughtfully. Fellowship with other believers, including someone more mature in faith. Such believers provide an example and are a source of encouragement.

Whatever you have to face this season, let me leave you with this straightforward reality:

Peace is not always a feeling, but it is a knowing.

It understands that even if we don't figure out the "whys" behind what we're going through right now, we do know that the God who holds the universe in the palm of His hands is more than enough to love us, and, He's in control. He has vowed never to leave or forsake you (Hebrews 13:5) ... If you have nothing else to hold onto for hope today, hold onto that. He is by your side, and He cares.

"God takes us down paths we never want to travel and roads we never want to see to get us to a place we never want to leave."

Unknown

Keep on Keeping On...

Lord, sometimes life feels too problematic, and nothing makes sense, help me fix my eyes on You. Like the songwriter who said, "Roll back the curtains of memory now and again," Lord, please continue to remind me that You can bring good from even the worst situations. I will continue to choose to rely on Your unfailing love. In Jesus' name, Amen.

The turmoil we face comes from the devil because there is no truth in him. He is a prevaricator and a crook, and then he will always try to distract, confound, and deceive us. We can conquer this turmoil through the Word and the Blood of our beloved Lord and Savior, Jesus Christ. There is so much proof that God has already won the war. There is so much proof in his Word that He commanded us to feed on like newborn babies.

1 John 3:8 states, "For this purpose, the Son of God was manifested, that He might destroy the works of the devil."

God is a God of declarations. He established the universe and the laws of science that hold everything in place. He gave us His Word, and He gave us peace.

1 Corinthians 14:33 confirms, "For God is not the author of confusion, but of peace, as in all churches of the saints."

We must not permit ourselves to focus on the chaos or the lies but look instead to the author and finisher of our faith. Jesus spent little time being diverted by the works of the devil...in fact, He would not authorize the demons even to speak but commanded them to "hold their peace" or not to say forth things that would add confusion.

Luke 4:35 states, "And Jesus rebuked him, saying, hold thy peace, and come out of him. And when the devil had thrown him in the midst, he went out of him and hurt him not."

When confusion comes in, we must take authority over the chaos by pleading with the Blood of Jesus Christ and by standing on what God promises us as believers in Him. We must be fierce in our battle against confusion, as Paul states...

2 Corinthians 10:3-5 declares, "For though we walk in the flesh; we do not war after the flesh. (For the weapons of our warfare are not carnal,

but mighty through God to the pulling down of strong holds;) Casting down imaginations (word-for-word – confused thoughts), and every high thing that exalted itself against the knowledge of God, and bringing into captivity every thought to the obedience of Christ."
We should not worry about this battle but know that there is love, power, and clarity through Christ.

2 Timothy 1:7 reminds us, "For God hath not given us the spirit of fear; but of power, love, and a sound mind."

Praying in the Spirit enables us to accentuate these times of confusion because when we do not know not what to pray, the Spirit will intercede for us. When God is all you acquire, you'll understand that God is all you desire.

Jesus' devotion to you and I do not depend on our level of perfection. He wants us to surrender to Him perfectly.

Times of turmoil can shake us, especially if our faith is not fervent. God has been a God for a long time and will always be God. Seasons change. However, our God does not change. He does not work based on how we feel, nor does He work by our emotions. He does not need to work based on our timeline. The words He spoke over your life will not return to him void. He knows what He is doing. He will do all He has to get you to your purpose.

When God has a plan for your life, it will be fulfilled. He will do everything to get you to where He needs you to be.

I wanted to move back home in June 2020. I applied to every company I knew I could get a job with; however, because of the pandemic, someone else was hiring. Even then, I was determined to move back home. I believe God would work it out if it were His will. I knew it would be challenging because I still struggled even with a full-time job. I can only imagine what it would be like without a steady income. I was just tired. My life had hit a big stop, and nothing seemed to work. I just wanted to go home.

Do you believe God places people in our lives for a reason and sometimes for a particular season? Have you ever looked at your life and wondered what God is doing? We should never doubt what God is doing. I have tried to steer my life how I think it should be multiple times, and God keeps shifting it to how He knows it should be. Most times, we need help understanding certain situations. But if we pray about it, He will reveal it to us. I prayed about my situation, asking God what to do. I wanted to stay as I met someone and would like to date for the first time in over ten years, which is very rare, but; that was one of the reasons I wanted to move back home. I was lonely and needed my family.

During that season of my life, a friend of mine encouraged me to reapply to stay a bit longer as she knew it would be approved. She said her faith would cover my fears. I pondered for a year what I should do as I knew it would only be agreed upon with the necessary paperwork. My mind was in a state of turmoil. On the one hand, I wanted to stay and date this young man I met in April of that year, which coincidently would give my daughter time also to finish high school, and on the other hand, I felt it was time to go. I had overstayed my welcome.

But I was reminded that God was in control the day I submitted the documents. God's Word is guaranteed. We can feel comforted knowing that Jesus is still on the throne and spending time in prayer is very necessary. Not only was the document submitted, but it was approved. I remember praying and crying, asking God will this even be supported. I can't see how. While praying, I heard I have never failed you. I will make a way. I always do.

I realized prayer is one way we can express trust in God. He also promises that He hears our prayers. Psalm 116:1–2 says, "I love the Lord because He has heard my voice and my pleas for mercy. Because

He inclined His ear to me, I will call on Him as long as I live." We can have confidence that God hears our prayers and that nothing can separate us from the love of Christ.

The practice of praying has many different facets. You can pray off the cuff, you can pray Bible verses, you can pray prayers of the church, or you can pray from prayers already written down. And it would be best if you tried doing all of them.

"When our children see us clinging to the promises of God, they will grow up trusting in His goodness. If we fail as adults praying for and praying with the next generation, they will become spiritually unsure".

Michael Youssef

Standing on God's Promises

Dear Lord, you came to set me free. To show me that not even death can defeat me. This pain I am going through is as temporary as a season and part of your fantastic tapestry of life. Can you reach mightily into my plight and offer relief? Can you visit me with renewed strength, soft wisdom, and a stirring of hope?

I ask for your intervention. Although I know you will amaze me in time, I am a very deficient spirit. Please, God, raise me. Please send me a ray of sunshine. Please heal my broken heart. In Jesus' name, amen.

We do not fight for victory; we fight from victory—Christ has already had the final word over our enemy. But because we are human, we still find ourselves distressed and need firm faith.

"A woman who fought her way through adversity became an inspiration for many people who watched her journey."

"She was a magnificent example of an overcomer. Unfortunately, no one knew her troubles as she kept a happy smiling face for the public. I can't imagine what demons drove her to feel that her only option was ending her life. My thoughts are now with her family, especially her one-year-old daughter".

"I have no words. May her family find a resolution in this dark time. May we all find peace of mind in our everyday lives. Every day is winding; you may never know who is on edge. Many of us can't process emotions and how to deal with them".

These are a few quotes I always imagined would be said after October 25, 2007, the day I took my life. You see, I had just experienced my first heartbreak. But the truth be told, it was not so much the heartbreak that caused me to want to terminate my life. It was the fact that I had to be a single mom. That was something I never wanted to experience. I was a confused, naive, gullible girl who was too scared to face the uncertainty of life.

I merely completed two years into my career. I was a devoted nurse still attending college to get a second degree in Education. Just minutes before taking my life. I just started to pray and cry to God for forgiveness and tell Him why this was easier for me. This is the best route to take, I thought. It eliminates so much of what I may face in the future. God knew I never wanted to be a single mom. That is one of the reasons why I had a pregnant pause about having my daughter. The fact that I was scared to be like my mom. Raising children alone.

Most of my family members are single parents. I always thought this was a generational curse in my family.

Generational influences can bring blessings – or curses – to your life. This lesson stuck out to me the most from Sunday school. An understanding brings the power to change not only your life but the lives of your family members.

Family is important to God, and it is clear that He does not think merely in terms of individuals but also in terms of generations. Matthew 1:17 tells us: "So all the generations from Abraham to David are fourteen generations, from David until the captivity in Babylon is fourteen generations, and from the captivity in Babylon, until the Christ are fourteen generations."

When God looks at you, He also sees your family. He sees where you came from. He looks at your ancestors, and He looks at your children and grandchildren.

When making a covenant with Abraham, God never once said, "I'm going to bless you." He always said, "I will bless you and your descendants." An example is Genesis 22:17-18, where God said, "In blessing, I will bless you, and multiplying I will multiply your descendants as the stars of heaven and as the sand which I seashore; and your descendants shall possess the gate of their enemies. In your seed, all the nations of the earth shall be blessed because you have obeyed My voice."

Abraham obeyed God and was blessed, and his descendants were blessed, too, because blessings tend to run along bloodlines.

Many people, if not most, can identify some symptoms passed on from generation to generation. How about you? When you look at your family tree, do you see a pattern?

Do you struggle with a particular sin and see a history of that sin in past generations? Maybe you've been told that the depression or fear you deal with runs in the family, or perhaps you struggle with marital infidelity. You can identify a pattern of affairs and divorce going back to a parent and grandparent. These could be symptoms of a generational curse.

Earlier in my walk with God, I prayed that every generational curse would end with me, and I continue to declare it is broken.

> ***Thank you, God; those generational curses are broken through faith in the blood of Jesus. I put my trust in the blood. I believe Jesus is my mercy seat, and His blood cancels the curse and breaks generational iniquities. By the blood of Jesus, I know the generational curse from the law is canceled and broken off my family now, in Jesus' name. Thank you that sins, bondages, and iniquities are blotted out, and the blood of Jesus stops the curse. Thank God that the blood of Jesus on the mercy seat is a barrier against any nemesis, In Jesus' name. Amen.***

"There is hope, even when your brain tells you there isn't."

John Green

A Change of Heart

Father God, the darkness has taken hold of me, and I can't find my way back to the light. At this moment, ending it all seems like the best option, the only option, the only way to escape. Yet, something in me wants your light to snuff out the darkness. So, I ask, Lord, that you would do just that. You are the only light that can shine in the dark.

When I'm consumed with thoughts of death, I believe lies from the enemy. I ask you to remind me of these truths: when I feel alone, you are with me; when I feel invisible, you see me; when I feel worthless, my value is knowing and being known by you. Lord, help me understand that you are enough because you are everything I need. Remind me that you have hope in me and for me when I feel hopeless. Remind me that when I don't have the words to cry out to you, your son Jesus is praying for me, and your Spirit intercedes for me with groanings too deep for words. This reminds me that I am seen, heard, and deeply loved.

I often feel out of place in this world. I don't fit in, and I'm not sure I want to. Remind me that this world is not my home, and while, as your child, I will never fit in here, my time here isn't over. Not yet. Please, give me the desire to live in Jesus' name. Amen.

While praying to God that dark day in October 2007, I heard the voice so clearly telling me to read Isaiah 54. I flew up so fast and circled the house several times to see if it was someone outside mocking me. I had wandered so far away from God that I forgot His voice. When I read the scriptures of the Bible verse. I wailed like a woman travailing in a child's birth. Indeed, this was the Son of God. I sat and read each verse. My resolve was unmistakably clear. I had to live as God has a purpose for my life. Looking back on my life, I've cried so many tears over loves that didn't work out and had my heart broken countless times, and it just seemed so unfair why everyone else could have love, yet it eluded me.

I grew apart from once close friends and lost touch with others along the way.

Life seemed unjust in the way it worked out for some and not for others.

Or so I thought.

That's when I realized I was exactly where I was supposed to be all along.

I may not have gotten everything I wanted, but I always seemed to get what I needed by the grace of God.

It hurts so badly when a relationship doesn't work out, but later, I always understood why it didn't because I knew it was for the best.

For them, I kept pushing forward to where I was supposed to be, closer to God. God wanted me to have a relationship with Him first. He wanted to be my first love.

All the things I thought "weren't working out for me" were helping me to become the person I needed to be while drawing closer to God.

I needed broken hearts to understand real love.

I needed to lose friends to appreciate the ones close to my heart.

I needed to struggle to enjoy my victories.

I wasn't always given what I wanted, but I always got what I needed. There's been so many days that I wanted to quit and other times when I thought I could conquer the world.

That's the beauty of this life we are given- to appreciate the ups and downs, to understand what is essential, and most of all, to value the things that matter most.

So, while I still have bad days and people sometimes vanish from my life, I know it's for the greater good to help me learn, evolve, and grow.

Change can be painful, but staying in a place not meant for you is even worse.

I may not always know why, but I'll end up where I'm meant to be through God's grace, power, and might.

I always believed true love would find me when it was time, and in the meantime, I'll keep posture in the waiting room.:

And if it never happens when I expect God to bless me, I know He will do it in His time.

What's meant to be will always find a way, in whichever way is meant for me.

So, I'll keep moving forward with my warrior spirit,

Every day, in every way, with everything I've got.

So, while I may not have all the answers or know what tomorrow will bring, I'm happy living each day to its fullest- because God is with me and for me, and no one can stand against me.

For all its beautiful moments, tragedies, and triumphs.

And the love I feel in my heart every day.

A whole heart and a content soul will always be enough to make me happy.

On my way to becoming the person I'm meant to be. Because with God, all things are possible.

> ***God, you knew me before I was born. I do not know everything about myself, but You do. Touch my heart. Let it be more like you. Hold me when I am about to fall off that cliff called life. Breathe over my situation. Breathe life back into my body. You are God. You have been God for a long time. Seasons change, but you do not change. You have been for a long time, and you will always be God. My provider, my healer, my defender, My God. Help me to continue trusting You with my life in Jesus' name. Amen.***

"If I am perturbed by the reproach and misunderstanding that may follow action taken for the good of souls for whom I must give account; if I cannot commit the matter and go on in peace and silence, remembering Gethsemane and the cross, then I know nothing of Calvary love."

Amy Carmichael

Making a Commitment to God

Lord God, please forgive me for everything I have done wrong. I turn to you and turn away from sin. Jesus, please be the center of my life. I welcome you personally as the Lord and Savior of my life. I ask you, Holy Spirit, to fill me and empower me to live as a child of God. I want your grace to live a new life genuinely; thank you for hearing my prayer through Christ our Lord. Amen.

Recovering from heartbreak will look different for everyone. Remember to be compassionate to yourself. Heartbreak does not have to be from a relationship. It may be the loss of a family member, coworker, or friend. It can even be the loss of a job, contract, or promotion you had expected. Whatever makes your heart ache, remember to show yourself the same love and patience you would like a friend.

Some days praying for a broken heart will take real discipline, while it will come quickly for others. Have grace for the days you don't manage it, and remember that healing can take time.

God is passionate about you; He loves you deeply and plans to prosper you. No matter the depth of your pain, you can put your faith in a God whose love for you will not be shaken.

God's grace is more than impressive. It is God's unmerited favor freely bestowed on all who believe.

At the age of thirteen, God told me (not a prophet or minister) that I was a uniquely chosen vessel. He had handpicked me to use for His glory. I knew God placed a call on my life, but I had compromised it, resulting in me walking in disobedience.

How grateful am I today!

Nothing can stand in God's way. No one. Not even you. Not even me. Not even that enemy, compulsion, or circumstance seeking to take you down. Nothing can thwart God's plan because, as the Scripture says, "He does whatever He pleases" (Psalm 115:3).

Now, you can be on the good side of God's sovereignty or the wrong side of God's power. That doesn't change His sovereignty. It just changes your personal experience of it. It's like when a parent tells a teenager, "We can make this easy, or we can make it hard that's up to you." The teenager's choices will impact how the parents teach the lesson they are trying to convey. And while your actions never determine God's providence, your actions influence how efforts providence come to light in your life.

God's plans may be made manifest with your cooperation, or they may be made manifest despite your rebellion. Regardless, His pathways and dreams will come about. God knows that whichever direction you go on the path He's placed before you, He will get you to His intended destination. Now, due to your own choices, that may mean delays and treacherous treks— or even, like Moses, the loss of realizing the experience of the dream (Deuteronomy 34:4). But He will keep pointing you in the direction He desires until His sovereign rule is achieved.

"Amazing grace! How sweet the sound that saved a wretch like me! I once was lost, but now I am found; I was blind, but now I see".

John Newton

God's Amazing Grace

Father in heaven comforts the hearts of everyone struggling to stay afloat. Heal the heart of those who are suffering from any affliction. Set them free from the strongholds of the adversary. Let your face shine upon them and give them peace. The kind of peace that surpasses human understanding. In Jesus' name. Amen.

We often build walls around our hearts to protect ourselves from pain and suffering. Because I had been a victim of abuse, I did not trust people or God to protect me, so subconsciously I spent many years building defense mechanisms to protect myself. But to step into the destiny God had planned and prepared for me, I had to allow the Holy Spirit to do deep work inside.

I learned that God wanted to take my hard heart and make it tender to fulfill His purposes in my life. I had to learn to trust God and trust people. I had to lose control and learn how to feel again. This was the most painful process of my life.

But as I committed to healing and restoration, I discovered that our heavenly Father is loving, kind, compassionate, and gracious. In His tender mercy and endless patience, He proved to me time and time again that He is faithful. And He is devoted to you too! Hand over your prison key to Jesus and allow Him to do what He can.

I used to wonder why Jesus told us to ask, seek, and knock. Didn't God know what we wanted? Can't He give us what we want? It is pretty simple: He understands that humans take things they acquire quickly for granted.

We need to grasp the truth that faith is active instead of passive. Faith is not about sitting still and not doing anything. The Bible clearly says that faith without works is dead. Faith is the language of God's Kingdom. God responds to our faith; He longs to relate with us as a Father relates to His children.

Our patience, honesty, perseverance, and character are tested as we ask, seek, and knock. Can we bear long suffering, or do we easily give up? We will discover strengths to cultivate, old habits to let go of, things we can do, and things beyond our capabilities. We will find the people who are faithful to us and gain experience, wisdom, and insight as we journey through the opened door.

He (Jesus) replied, "Because the knowledge of the secrets of the kingdom of heaven has been given to you, but not to them" (Matthew 13:11). This is one of our privileges as children of God. The word 'secrets' originated from 'mysterion' (a mystery or hidden thing). Secrets don't stroll in public places; therefore, we must search for them. God won't require us to ask, seek, and knock if there is nothing for us to find in the first place; or if He hasn't provided us with what is good; and if the door won't be opened for us.

> ***Father, thank you for being my safe place -I know I can talk about anything with You. I'm grateful I can confidently ask You for the things I need, seek You consistently, and ask You for things that seem impossible. You are a miracle-working God—and I am honored to trust You with my life. In Jesus' name, Amen.***

"Every great journey begins with one step, and it begins with moving forward. Remember, going through pain is temporary, and it will subside."

Louie Herron

Guard against Setbacks

Father, by the anointing, break every yoke of stagnation and setbacks standing against the glorious destiny of your children and cause them to go forward in the name of Jesus. Father, by your word, I command every red sea standing as an instrument of stagnation and setback for your people to go forward to part way in the name of Jesus.

Our backs are not meant to hold the weight, worries, and chaos of this life. Prayer puts these burdens back on the One who can, will, and wants to bear this weight. The One—that has the solution and sees every detail, and knows the perfect outcome.

In the years that followed my attempted suicide, I told myself it was the grief and shame of being a single parent that breathed too much to survive. That was the reason I wanted to kill myself.

I thought my life would be different after the incident. I thought it would be wholesome. But the trials and struggles came in like a flood—setbacks after setbacks. I look to other things for sources of strength. My focus was still not on God.

I loved God, but I never truly gave Him a first place at that juncture. Peering back twenty-one years ago, I shouldn't have wandered away from Him. To be out of God and Christ is the most disastrous mistake one can ever make.

When your load becomes so heavy that it affects you mentally, emotionally, and physically, you may need to look for ways to rearrange the load.

Moses' most important weapon against setbacks was his ongoing dialogue with God. Moses suffered a temporary setback because of reasons that could not be labeled spiritual. If we fail to see that our physical, mental, and emotional condition makes us more vulnerable to satan's attacks, then the enemy has already won the battle.

Long before you face a problem, God already has a strategy. I toiled with my faith in God after that incident. I am not where I want to be even presently, but I am nowhere I was twenty-one years ago. I have learned that the only way God can demonstrate He's the regulator of our life is to put us in predicaments we can't rectify. Sometimes God doesn't take our trials away but reaches us through them.

The Creator will fulfill good even when life doesn't look promising or feel promising. Even if we can't discern it, I trust we'll choose to believe it. Romans 8:28 says, " And we know that in all things God works for the good of those who love him, who have been called according to his purpose."

"God delights in seeing you transformed and becoming more like Him."

Bobby Gene Redding

Steadfast in Faith

Lord, open the eyes of my heart. Heal my shortsightedness, my farsightedness, and the astigmatism of my soul. I want to see all things from your perspective, including the hope to which you have called us. To see with eyes of hope means that I will be able to discern your heart and hand at work everywhere. Amen.

During my teenage year, I was a victim of rape. I remember him telling me he would throw me over the bridge in my community as he believed I would tell people about it and get him in trouble. I cried for what seemed like the entire evening. Telling him, I would not. He said he did not believe me. I told him I wouldn't. How afraid I was of dying. I even promised to have a relationship with him, fearing that he might kill me if he believed I would tell someone. I was never the same after that day. I stopped sitting in the choir and participated in church. I just gave up and sat in the back row of the church.

I wished I knew then that storms in life are unavoidable, rather than jumping ship, walking away from God, and backsliding. I should have clung to God and faced my future with grit.

Backsliding is a uniquely biblical word. Jeremiah 2:19, God says, "Your wickedness will correct you, and your backslidings will rebuke you. Know therefore and see that it is an evil and bitter thing that you have forsaken the Lord your God...." Also, Jeremiah 3:22 says, "Return, you backsliding children, and I will heal your backsliding."

The Bible tells the story of a man who backslides, someone whom no one probably expected to fall away. It is the story of Simon Peter and his denial of Jesus Christ. Peter had walked with the Lord during three years of intensive discipleship, and yet Peter denied Him. It is a reminder to us that any of us have the potential to fall.

Peter's denial was not merely a spontaneous response to unexpected danger or embarrassment. For all practical purposes, he had already laid out the groundwork for desertion. No one suddenly backslides. A series of steps always lead to it because we either build up or weaken our spiritual character daily. We are either moving forward or falling backward.

Do uncertainty, distrust, and insecurity afflict you right now? The adversary has been wreaking confusion on your mind, heart, and soul.

I felt prompted to remind you that God has not given you a spirit of fear, but love, power, and a sound mind. God is for you and not against you. God is with you and has not forsaken you. You haven't deterred your purpose, and the devil doesn't have the power to steal it from you. Although the weapon has been forged against you, it shall not prevail. It is not over. You're not finished. Don't relinquish. Don't quit. The devil is a liar. God's promises are yea and amen over your life. Continue to hold on to God. He will never leave or forsake you. Just continue to trust Him.

"When you have a setback, it is a setting forth of great you and greater things for you in the future."

Aiyaz Uddin

Pray Against Setbacks

Heavenly Father. Let this fear fall away, as my heart desires to seek You, for You are the rock of my life, fortress, and strength, even when I am weak. Help me to be confident in all situations, knowing that You hold the future and trusting that everything works together for my good. Amen.

We serve a God who can never be too early or too late; He is always on time. No matter the situations and circumstances you may be going through today, I want you to know that God will deliver you and deliver on time. His timing is not usually ours; you may be thinking," my friend has gotten so and so, but I am still without," but God sent me to tell you today that your miracle is on the way, and it will come on time. Not all setbacks are normal; some are demonic-oriented, so you should always be in prayer.

In the Book of Daniel 10:13, Daniel's prayers were delayed for twenty-one days by the Prince of Persia; Daniel got the victory because He persisted in his prayers. We must understand that spiritual forces are out there to delay our breakthroughs; they try to resist our prayers by attacking our faith. But as we pray these strong, no more delayed prayer points today, every resistance on your path to your breakthroughs shall be crushed permanently in Jesus' name.

In Luke 18:1, Jesus said we should always pray and not faint. Persistent prayers are the antidote for the spirit of delays. You shall never lose in Jesus' name when you pray. You must continually resist the devil in prayers to see your answers delivered. This no more delay prayer points will end delays in your life forever in Jesus' name. It doesn't matter how impossible your situation may seem; the God that raised Lazarus from the dead will lift you out of that challenge to your promised land in Jesus' name. Use these prayer points with faith today and see God bring you your long-awaited testimonies.

1. I break the curses of the spirit of the frustrations over my life in the name of Jesus.

2. The blood of Jesus nullifies every effect of the spirit of the delays over my life.

3. Every spirit of slow progress and stagnation in my life receives the fire of God now and is destroyed in the name of Jesus.

4. Every spirit of avoiding good things in my life is destroyed in the name of Jesus.

5. O Lord, I reject carry-over curses in my life in Jesus' name

6. I will not feed from waste bins of life in the name of Jesus.

7. I refuse to have the leftover of life in the name of Jesus.

8. Every spirit of irritation in my life, be washed off by the blood of Jesus.

9. I reject the spirit of fear, anxiety, and discouragement in the name of Jesus.

10. Every evil instruction, prophecy, or prediction issued against my life by demonic utterances be canceled by the blood of Jesus.

Pray these prayer points repeatedly because God has already given you victory.

"God knows our situation; He will not judge us as if we had no difficulties to overcome. What matters is the sincerity and perseverance of our will to overcome them."

C.S. Lewis

Glamorizing Christianity

God, I don't want to be irresponsible, so help me to concentrate on your promises. This walk with you is very burdensome. I want to submit fully to your will and surrender to you daily. I want to always be in alignment with your Will. Vanquish all things from my purview that distract me and compete for my attention. Instead, allow me to focus solely on the task at hand so I may be pleasing to You. Amen

For a few years, I thought my daughter was an atheist. I had failed as a mom and someone who spent all her years trying to do the right thing; this was the epitome of failure in my book.

Her statements would puzzle me, and all I would do was pray about it. Because what else can I do? And one of the things that the Holy Spirit revealed to me was to be practical with her in my walk with God.

For a long while, my task in our nightly devotion was to share my experiences and struggles with my daily walk with Christ. As best as possible, stop pretending that I am not in the bathroom crying, stop praying in my mind, and be open with her.

It is a guarantee without a shadow of a doubt that we will have trouble in this world as Jesus himself did. It is impossible to live in this world and not have concerns. But, with His power and presence in our lives, we are called to endure and thus shine the light of Christ in a dark world.

Do you know someone who has just started their walk with God? Be a mentor for that person. Let that person know that this walk they will embark on is tough. The trials are going to come. Destruction won't stop. It will be one of the most challenging roads they have probably ever walked. But if they stay in alignment with God. It will be rewarding. Don't tell them this walk with Jesus is easy because it is not. They have to purpose in themselves daily that this is what they want to do and nothing else matters except living a life that pleases God. That is the conversation we need to have with our minted Christian converts.

Testing of your faith defines the meaning of a trial for the Christian: Jesus was "tested" in the wilderness (Matt. 4:1–13), so believers are tested. The result is steadfastness, a life of faithful endurance amid troubles and afflictions.

Steadfastness leads ultimately to perfection. Believers grow in holiness but need to be perfected in it; such embodiment will be realized only when Jesus returns.

Christians need not fear the devil, for the Lord has given them the power to stand against him by being firm in their faith. Trusting in God's promises, believers know that suffering is not the final word and that, ultimately, they will be exalted.

Though suffering will come first, it will be followed by eternal glory. The God who effectually called believers by His grace will fortify us with His strength so they can endure.

"Simply put, to please God means to bring Him delight by being and doing what He desires."

Robert D. Jones

The Great Counselor

Thank You, Lord, for the humble example of Moses as he received Godly counsel. Help me grow in faith so I can respond with wisdom, gentleness, and teachability to words that flow from Your Truth. I pray in the name of Jesus. Amen.

Moses was tired. He was trying to do it all—be the leader of Israel and countless other duties. One of his responsibilities was to be the nation's judge over personal disputes.

When Jethro, Moses's father-in-law, caught up with him at Mount Sinai, he could not believe what he saw. To say that Moses's time was spread thin is a gross understatement. He was one step away from mental and emotional burnout. We read that Jethro wasted no time in talking to Moses about this:

When his father-in-law saw all Moses was doing for the people, he said, "What is this you are doing for the people? Why do you alone sit as a judge while all these people stand around you from morning till evening?" Moses answered him, "Because the people come to me to seek God's will. Whenever they have a dispute, it is brought to me, and I decide between the parties and inform them of God's decrees and instructions." (Exodus_18:14-16)

Jethro quickly discerned the Truth—Moses had taken on more than God intended. Therefore, he encouraged Moses to appoint judges to handle lesser disputes. He also admonished Moses to teach God's people the Lord's decrees and laws and show them how to live (Exodus 18:20). In other words, Moses needed to teach the people what God desired and how to take responsibility for their actions before the Lord. Are you willing to accept godly counsel?

When Moses heard Jethro's words, he knew his father-in-law was right, and he was not too proud to accept his advice.

I remember traveling on the bus one evening, coming from work. If a seat is available in the back, I always sit there. I tried to get away from people as much as possible and wallow in my misery. A woman sat beside me, and I was pretty irate because of all the places to sit; why did she sit beside me? I had a colorful vocabulary, and I did not waste a minute telling her how I felt about her sitting beside me when so many seats were empty. She smiled, looked at me again, and smiled. I was taken aback. She said, “When I saw you on the bus, I saw you standing around an area with blocks, and as soon as I saw you standing there. All the blocks started to crumble”. She smirked and continued, “Is that your life? Everything just crumbling? In life, you need people. God places people in your life to help you, but you continue to refuse the help. God wants you to know I send these people to help you”.

Always be sure that what you hear from others is in line with the Word of God. Listen, pray, and ask God to confirm what has been suggested. The Lord will guide you when you seek His wisdom. The Lord God is our first counselor.

"Every person who has grown to any degree of usefulness, who has grown to distinction, almost without exception, has been a person who had risen by overcoming obstacles, removing difficulties, and resolving that when he met discouragement, he would not give up."

Booker T. Washington

The Twin Pillars

God, arise and let all the enemies of my breakthrough be scattered, destroyed, and buried forever in the name of Jesus.

Let Your fire melt away the stones hindering my blessings in the mighty name of Jesus. Oh God, let every evil cloud blocking my progress roll out now. All secrets of the enemy in the camp of my life that are still in the darkness allowed them to be exposed to me now, in Jesus' name. Amen

Delay and discouragement are twins.

The prince of Persia was a spirit of delay against the destiny of Daniel.

Daniel 10:12-13 NLT – Then he said, "Don't be afraid, Daniel. Since the first day you began to pray for understanding and to humble yourself before your God, your request has been heard in heaven. I have come in answer to your prayer.[13] But for twenty-one days, the spirit prince[a] of the kingdom of Persia blocked my way. Then Michael, one of the archangels,[b] came to help me, and I left him there with the spirit prince of the kingdom of Persia".

I studied how the spirit of delay manifests itself:

– Fear

Daniel 10:12a – Then he said, "Don't be afraid, Daniel…

The fear of never achieving one's purpose in life can creep into the heart when there is a delay.

We see this in the life of Abram and his wife, Sarah. They had waited long to have a child and were now old and beyond average child-bearing age. Abram's response indicated fear that he would never father a child…

Genesis 15:1-3 – After these things, the word of the Lord came to Abram in a vision, saying, "Do not be afraid, Abram, I am your shield, your exceedingly great reward."

But Abram said, "Lord GOD, what will You give me, seeing I go childless, and the heir of my house is Eliezer of Damascus?" Then Abram said, "Look, you have given me no offspring; indeed, one born in my house is my heir!"

Delay can result in self-effort if allowed.

Self-effort is an intentional manipulation of one's destiny. It shows a lack of trust in God and disrespect for who God is.

John 15:5 NLT – "Yes, I am the vine; you are the branches. Those who remain in me, and I in them, will produce much fruit. For apart from me, you can do nothing...."

Abraham and Sarah chose to "do something" to make things happen for themselves.

Write this down and recite it: Self-effort always cultivates a momentary fix but leads to eternal sorry.

In Exodus 32, The children of Israel built a golden calf to be their God and object of worship because Moses delayed coming down from Mt. Sinai...

This infuriated God, and you know the story – all of that generation except two – Joshua and Caleb's bands made it into the promised land. Knowing that self-effort can never accomplish God's design for you is essential. His design came from His thoughts, which are higher than ours – Isaiah 55:9.

Revelation 10:6 expresses the mind of God for His own:

"...And he swore by him who lives forever and ever, who created the heavens and all that is in them, the earth and all that is in it, and the sea and all that is in it, and said, "There will be no more delay! "

Habakkuk 2:3 – The revelation awaits an appointed time; it speaks of the end and will not prove false. Though it lingers, please wait for it; it will certainly come and will not delay.

Since Fear is the opposite of faith, and without it, it is impossible to please God (Hebrews 11:6), fear permits the devil to prevail. Don't be afraid to face and overcome fear in the place of prayer, for God has not given us the spirit of fear but of power, love, and a sound mind – 2 Timothy 1:7

Discouragement is a loss of confidence or enthusiasm; dispiritedness. In His Word, God expressed His will for us in Deuteronomy 31:6 – "Be strong and courageous, do not be afraid or terrified because of them, for the Lord your God goes with you; he will never leave you nor forsake you."

If left to fester, discouragement is hazardous and can lead to the abortion of plans and destiny. Some commit suicide, and others, murder, because of discouragement.

David's men were discouraged and wanted to stone him at Ziklag (read 1 Samuel 30).

Though David also was greatly distressed, the Bible says: …but David encouraged himself in the Lord His God (1 Samuel 30:6)

No matter how long you have waited for the promise of God, never allow discouragement to quench the hope God has placed inside of you. But through patience, wait to inherit the promise!

One of the most significant battles we face as believers are discouragement. We become discouraged when we meet unmet expectations: the relationship ends, the promotion needs to be achieved, the school doesn't accept us, and the list goes on. To get discouraged means to remove courage. When we lack courage, we get paralyzed by fear and worry. The result is a detour in our destiny. We live in a place of delay, never moving forward into God's purpose and plans for our lives.

A few years ago, ok...a very long time ago, I wanted to be a doctor; however, my mom could not send me to medical school because we did not have the money. It was a significant discouragement for me, a major delay. At the same time, my friends lost their newborn babies. We were all devastated. During this season, I felt my life was being overtaken by discouragement. I had a choice. I could sit back and embrace it or take the same action David took throughout the Psalms.

Discouragement will inevitably come, but we have a choice when it does. What do we do when we become discouraged? One of the greatest weapons we have when facing discouragement is the one David excelled in worship. The psalmist David wrote, "Praise the Lord, oh my soul." In the time of worship, we "forget not all His benefits." When we are reminded of what God has done, we remove the frustration of what we don't see happening. Worship is a weapon that lets us focus on how good God is instead of how discouraging life can be.

What benefits can we focus on that we receive from God amid discouraging seasons?

David sums them up for us:

- "Who forgives all your sins"-Forgiveness

- "Heals all your diseases"-Healing

- "Redeems your life from the pit"- Redemption

"Crowns you with love and compassion"-Purpose.

If you are facing discouragement today, fight the battle with the weapon of worship. Praise God for what he has done, and watch how your discouragement is turned into courage, your fear is turned into faith, and your anxiety is turned into peace. When we worship, our focus moves from what is not happening to what God has already done.

Abiding in Jesus isn't fixing our attention on Christ, but it is one with Him ... A man is enduring just as much when he is sleeping for Jesus as when he is awake and working for Jesus. Oh, it is an adorable thing to have one's mind just resting there.

Author: Hudson Taylor

Abiding in Jesus

Living Lord, I am yours. I wear the helmet of salvation and hope. I carry the shield of faith and your word. I hold the sword of the spirit. I buckle the belt of truth around my waist. I put on the breastplate of righteousness and walk with the boots of readiness and peace. I am yours in Jesus' name, Amen.

For a long while, I was employed by this spirit as its right-hand man to drive people away and allow abandonment and isolation to move in. I felt like I was cursed with the spirit of rejection. I remember a prophet recounting what he saw in the spirit. He looked at me, and the word rejection was written on my forehead in significant, bold letters. However, that was not new, as that was how I felt. I have learned that delay is one of the many mechanisms of the adversary to impede us from fulfilling our God-ordained destiny in the time we have been given.

I've cried to God. I have tried and failed on every account in my life. He can do what seems fit in my life.

I told myself this spirit of rejection would taunt me with failure after another, hoping I would say, "I give up!"

I know how hard it is to be in a low place. Some days I can't see my way out of it. But there's always a way with God. I only needed to stay close to him. Stay close to people who love Him. They say time heals; this may be true, but only if healing is truly the goal. A few years ago, I rededicated my life to God.

I prayed I would not step out of God's will for my life this time. God's ways are sometimes opposite of what we want and expect. I have to stand in the mirror and remind myself. God is my provider. God's provision is always what I crave. God's provision safeguards my heart. I've learned to trust God when circumstances break my heart.

I know He has a plan, and it will be good in time. I cried over and over, telling God only His will. It does not matter how impatient I am or become. I only need His will to be done. God promises He can use my broken heart for good. And He is a God who keeps His promises. I dedicated my life to being more like Him. To live for him. For him to use me as He sees fit. It is easy to get discouraged in waiting seasons.

That is why I tried to inject the gap by declaring openly every hint of God's action in my life. I make a list and place it all over my room, acknowledging that just because God is silent in one area of my life doesn't mean He's quiet in every area.

The more we engage in awareness of seemingly small, moment-by-moment instructions from God, the more our thinking will start to line up with His. I continue to walk in God's truth. I feel as if; if I could only live for God. Do His will. I will make it to heaven. This is my only goal at this point in my life. I am living for Jesus.

We all have suffered troubles at one time or another. Some people handle them well, and others have never realized how to face them, nor do they try to discover how. God is concerned about how you endure them. Half the battle of life is learning how to face troubles. Jesus let you know when He was here that you would have problems in this world; He had many issues, and He met them head-on. He said in the world ye shall have tribulation: but be of good cheer; I have overcome the world (John 16:33). In the earth, you will have tribulation—trials—but through Jesus, you can be an overcomer. By living through and in Him to overcome all, you learn to face troubles when they come your way.

I've suffered a lot of depression because I couldn't face my problems. Although I didn't give up on God, the blows slowed me down in serving Him and seemed to take the very spirit out of me.

The secret I've learned of overcoming is facing problems head-on. Again and again, I am disappointed, but I don't bow down to them. I know the Lord will bring me out when I turn to Him.

My troubles stem from being made unhappy by the failures of desires and possibilities. I expect much from life and things to be just how I want. I anticipate God to answer prayers my way and answer them when I want them answered.

But God never promised to answer prayers my way instead of His. Over and over, I say, Lord, I want your will to be done, and then I am disappointed when it's different from my will. When I met the last person I dated, I prayed to God that if that's the one for me, let me know; if not, take that one away. God takes that person out of my life, and I am home crying and depressed with my face longer than a contrabandist's. Although I said, I wanted the will of God.

If you want the will of God but then are disappointed when you get it, you didn't like it. If you wish for the will of God, you will rejoice and praise Him for looking out for you. Some of us have landed in trouble by getting things we did not need—the wrong car, house, and companion. God, why didn't you do something? We cry.

Someone reminded me that God doesn't move for people in significant ways who live in bondages of disappointment. A spirit of disappointment can tow people down when they give in to it. Disappointment is like a millstone around their necks: "I'll never get anywhere. Life isn't good for me. This isn't the life the Lord promised". When you live with this type of spirit, you are not acknowledging God or walking with Him. To walk hand in hand with Jesus, you obey whatever He bestows you. In Job's hour of incredible suffering, Job said, " I know that my redeemer lives and that He shall stand at the latter day upon the earth: And after my skin worms destroy this body, yet in my flesh shall I see God" (Job 19:25,26). Job could have been disappointed; his wife certainly was. Her most helpful suggestion was: Curse God and die (Job 2:9).

Job recognized the foolishness of her words and reprimanded her for them. Job's wife was a curse to him because she did not have God in control. God didn't count on Job's wife, so God wasn't disappointed in her. He knew her spirit, knew all about her. God didn't ask, Hast thou considered my servant, Job's wife? God said Hast thou considered my servant Job, that there is none like him in the earth, a perfect and an upright man, one that feareth God, and eschewed evil (Job 1:8)? If you want God to say that about you, be prepared for the devil to rage.

Job's wife was disappointed in him; his friends were disappointed, but God wasn't. God turned Job's captivity into victory when he prayed for his disappointing friends, and the Lord gave Job twice as much as he had before (Job 42:10).

Disappointment breeds many problems, not the least of which is discouragement. The devil slows some people down in their work for God because they become discouraged when disappointment comes. The devil knows what will disappoint you, whether it's people or the lack of money, and he works to keep these areas stirred up for you. However, Jesus said not to let your heart be troubled: ye believe in God and me. In my Father's house are many mansions: if it were not so, I would have told you. I am going to prepare a place for you. And if I go and prepare a place for you, I will come again, and receive you unto myself; that where I am, ye may also be (John 14:1-3).

Don't let your heart be discouraged. Use this passage in John to cure your discouragement. When you get rid of the disappointments, the dismay will fade away. The blow can hit you for the moment—you are only human—but use the Word of God to rise above it all. All things work together for your good when you're plugged into Heaven with a standing order.

The spirit of rejection had me bound in a chain. I felt victimized, causing me to feel worthless and unwanted. But the word of God proved the truth in the end. He will give me a new beginning. He is rewriting my story. The past is the past. It is now time for the new.

"I find myself frequently depressed - perhaps more than anyone else here. And I find no better cure for that depression than to trust in the Lord with all my heart and seek to realize afresh the power of the peace-speaking blood of Jesus and His infinite love in dying upon the cross to put away all my transgressions."

Charles Spurgeon

A Biblical Prescription for Depression

Father, we come to You today touching and agreeing with anyone with hearts, minds, and spirits struggling to keep their heads above water. We ask in Your Name that You give them a refuge, a glimmer of hope, and a life-saving Word of Truth. We don't know every circumstance or situation they face, but Heavenly Father, You know. We cling to You with hope, faith, and assurance that You can heal our hurt places and pull us from the dark waters of depression and despair. We ask in Your Name that You allow those who need help to reach out to a friend, family member, pastor, counselor, or doctor.

We ask You to release the pride that may keep them from asking for help. May we all find our rest, strength, and sanctuary in You. Thank You for setting us free and giving us the glimmer of hope in living an abundantly entire life in Christ. Amen

Depression is genuine. It can cause us to feel isolated, alone, and hopeless...like everything around us is falling apart.

Satan uses depression to steal a person's spiritual power and freedom—he seeks to fill our minds with darkness and gloom and bring us down emotionally. However, God wants to help us live free from depression. He wants to supply us with His joy, hope, and expectation of good things for our lives.

An essential part of battling depression is winning the war over our feelings. We will always have feelings...they will never go away. However, we can make our emotions line up with our decisions.

When depression attacks, what we feel like doing is giving up. However, the way we respond to depression makes all the difference.

First, Peter 5:8-9 says to resist the devil at his onset. It's so important to resist the feeling of depression immediately because the longer we allow it to remain, the harder it is to fight!

We will deal with disappointments from time to time—that's a part of life. However, if we let it, our disappointment can lead to discouragement...and discouragement can lead to depression.

I've said this for years: If you don't let the devil impress you with what he does, then he can't oppress you; if he can't oppress you, he can't depress you. One of the most important things we can do is resist the devil at his onset!

I realize that depression may result from a physical or chemical imbalance, and I don't want to discount these causes. However, for many people, depression is a spiritual issue...and the Bible gives us great instructions on how to fight it.

Philippians 4:4 says, "Rejoice in the Lord always [delight, gladden yourselves in Him]; again I say, Rejoice!"

Praising the Lord amid our pain is the greatest thing we can do. Why? Because when we choose to fix our attention on God and rejoice in the good things He has done, we make Him more prominent than our problems.

I love Psalm 16:11. It says, "In your presence, there is fullness of joy; at your right hand are pleasures forever." When we worship God, we invite His presence into our lives. He replaces our discouragement and sadness with His joy and peace...giving us hope and breathing new life into our situation.

The mind is also a primary key to overcoming depression. Did you know that what you think about has the power to affect every area of your life? That's why renewing your mind with the promises found in God's Word is essential.

The more time you spend reading and thinking about His Word, the more it gets inside of you and begins to change you from the inside out. Hebrews 4:12 says God's Word "is alive and powerful" (NLT). It can change the way you see yourself and even your future. As you fill your mind with what God says about you and claim His promises as your own, it will bring hope and build your faith.

We can't control all of our circumstances, and we will never be completely free from experiencing pain or disappointment, but we don't have to let what happens today ruin tomorrow.

We have a choice. We can turn things around by deciding to let go of the situations that caused discouragement and depression and move toward the good things God has planned for our future.

Depression doesn't have to rule your life. No matter what you're going through, God is ready and willing to help you take your pain...and turn it into something extraordinary.

Often during this season, I asked the Lord for immediate restoration, but that was not his plan. Instead, it became increasingly clear that God was teaching me vital lessons for my stability in the faith. If you are in a similar season, please receive these gentle yet earnest exhortations.

Dwell in the Bible

When the blackness of spiritual depression is heavy upon your soul, you may not sense a hearty appetite for Scripture, but you must sit at the table anyway. While intentional Bible reading is not the only means God will use to lift the veil, it is indispensable and must be used with other means. Remember that David, who more than once cried out to God in mind-numbing despair, also confessed that God's word "restores the soul" (Psalm 19:7). To pursue a way out of your spiritual woes apart from Scripture will either lead to more significant trouble or set you on a trajectory of unstable experientialism. Remain in the Bible.

Abide in the Church

While walking through the thick haze of spiritual depression, I remember a friend who shared similar struggles, informing me that she was planning a month of shut-in to get alone with God. Although it sounded good at the time, I can confidently say that this friend's plan was wrongheaded and dangerous. Although time alone with Jesus is essential, our Savior does not intend to remedy our troubles by removing us from the community of believers. Instead, He has given our brothers, sisters, and pastors joy to help us persevere in the faith (Phil. 1:27; Heb. 3:12–15). During my despair, The Club House Social App was my church. I was able to be in prayer throughout the day every time I felt I was crumbling. There is always a room you can slide in to get peace for your situation; There is always a room where you can get mentorship, and there is always a room where you can request prayer. I thank

God for that great community. It saves me. I now have a church home, but I am on Club House every free time I get. Stay in the church.

Engage in the Gospel

When I say immerse yourself in the gospel, I mean primarily two things. First, do what you can to ground your mind and heart in the doctrine of justification. Dive into books to lift your faith in God. Read until you are convinced that you are in the right standing with God based on Christ's righteousness alone. (Rom. 4:5). Your spiritual troubles will likely remain to the degree that you are not resting in this foundational truth.

Secondly, seek to understand the doctrine of indwelling sin. When I was first converted, the depth and pervasiveness of my sin often staggered me. However, Colossians 3:1–11 and some solid counsel from Pastor Kelly brought lasting comfort to my soul. The truth I needed to hear was this: regeneration provides me with a new power to fight sin, not an immediate eradication of all my inward corruption. If you are unclear on this particular truth, you will be tossed to and fro by temptation and your sinful inclinations.

Pursue Means, Not Just Breakthroughs

While I don't think it is wrong to ask God for immediate breakthroughs of light into our spiritual darkness, I am convinced it is far better to seek means of gradual restoration. This approach is preferred because the constant desire for existential breakthroughs can unseat us from the sure rock of Scripture and draw us away from the disciplines God typically uses to grow and sustain our faith. God will often use the unheralded means of adequate sleep, exercise, a sensible diet, regular worship and fellowship, Bible reading, good books, time outdoors, faithfulness in our responsibilities, and thriving ministry to pull us out of the throes of spiritual depression.

Seek Obedience, Not Just Introspection

Those who tend toward spiritual depression often ruminate incessantly over the condition of their hearts. Some self-examination is excellent (2 Corinthians 13:5), but if we are not careful, self-examination can turn into morbid introspection, where we relentlessly appraise our motives and evaluate our affections; However, our reflection may appear super-spiritual, it might become a substitute for obedience. Instead of deleting that troublesome app and confessing your sin to a trusted friend, you look inside and ask, "Am I repentant over that recent indulgence in the work drama?" But God grants assurance not through introspection but through obedience. As you actively repent from known sin, you will find far more confidence and relief from depression than if you merely look inward for conclusive evidence that you love Jesus.

Keep Working

During my struggles, I was often convinced that time alone reading scripture, praying, and pouring over books was the only answer to my misery. Because of this, I often approached work as a hindrance to my spiritual health instead of what it was: a God-given means of renewal and stability. I would even ask my employer to grant me early leave from my workday so I could retreat to my home, close the door, and ponder over the troubles. It wasn't until I was forced into work situations that didn't allow withdrawals into my theological fantasyland that I started to see some break in the clouds. However, I found significant help in the simple means of a profitable workday. God made us work, and He intends that we see much physical and spiritual refreshment in attending diligently to our responsibilities.

Perform Your Ministry

The weight of life will often tempt us to fold in on ourselves. The remedy to our plight, however, is not more turning inward, but turning outward: first with faith in Jesus and the gospel, then to others in good works. You might feel unqualified to serve in ministry despite your spiritual troubles. But let your pastor make these decisions as you submit to His leadership, and commit to fulfilling your ministry. God has given you a spiritual gift to use for the good of the church (1 Corinthians 12:7), and you might be surprised by how the consistent use of your donation will set you on the path toward renewed joy and steadiness in the faith (see Paul's description of the faithful deacon in 1 Timothy 3:13).

Don't Cease in Movement

Those of us who tend toward spiritual depression may begin looking for a remedy that removes the need for further action on our part. The slowness of our recovery is the reason for more despair. But both of these tendencies obscure the truth that our Christian life is best likened to a marathon. Occasionally we may sense that we've hit our stride, but often we will enter stretches where the weight of our burden is enough to bring us to a crawl. But continue we must, for God has set along our course all the refreshment we need to remain in the race. Keep moving.

"Without worship, we go about miserable."

A. W. Tozer

The Art of Worship

Lord, I thank you that I can fear no evil because you are with me. Please help me to trust in your goodness and mercy every day of my life. Amen.

Worship is a heart response to who God is. It is the right and appropriate response to Jesus Christ, the Son of God - who Himself is God. How you respond to God in worship, despite your circumstances and despite anything that you stand to lose or gain, is evidence of your revelation of Him and your relationship with Him. When you are in His presence, the best response, without question, is always worship. Worship before any requests, even before your gifts or offerings (the wise men worshiped first before the presentation of skills). Worship without music, worship without words, worship when you feel like it, and worship when you don't - it is a matter of the heart to worship and to do so in spirit and truth.

Don't allow anything or anyone to limit your worship. Worship God whenever and wherever. Worship Him when you feel like it and even when you don't. Engage God in prayer daily, as worship is a critical tactic in spiritual warfare. Praising God helps us combat the enemy's lies and shut out that inner dialogue telling us we're not enough. It's impossible to focus on His goodness, faithfulness, power, and might while feeling weak, worried, afraid, or alone.

When people hear the word "worship," they think of the songs they sing in church or the music they hear on the local Christian radio station. But, by definition, worship is an expression of reverence and adoration for God. We worship when we give our tithe, serve with a joyful heart, show love to our neighbor, and help someone in need. Worship offers gratitude to God for who He is and what he has done.

I love how so many worship songs include God's word as song lyrics. It not only makes it easier to remember encouraging verses when we need them but just by singing, we can declare the truth of God's word over our situation. If you feel attacked at work and don't want to recite Bible verses or speak out against the enemy, you can boldly use your sword of the Spirit just by singing a few lines. Whether spoken or sung, keeping God's word on your lips throughout the day helps you stay in a mindset of worship.

We should always seek to honor God, but the road may not be easy. We may sometimes find ourselves in the "darkest valley" (Ps. 23:4). For example, in our workplaces, this could come as the loss of a contract, a teaching assignment that has gone bad, or feelings of isolation and meaninglessness. Or it could come as a longer-term struggle, such as a toxic office environment or inability to find a job. But Psalm 23 reminds us that God is near in all circumstances. His work on our behalf is not hypothetical but tangible and real. God will take care of us even in a sometimes-hostile world, "in the presence of my enemies" (Ps. 23:5). While we would often instead not think about this, it is through the challenges of our lives that God works out His purposes in us.

Psalm 23 my worship psalms conclude by reminding us of the destination of our journey with God: "I shall dwell in the house of the Lord forever" (Ps 23:6b). The first half of the verse tells us directly that this is a promise for our present lives as well as eternity: "Goodness and love will follow me all the days of my life" (Ps. 23:6a). The promise that God will be with us, bringing goodness and love into whatever circumstance we face. That is a deeper kind of comfort than we can ever get from, hoping to avoid every adversity that could befall us.

In many cases, we will never find a precise reason for our problems. But the good news is that God can and will use it for good in our lives if we let him. Worship can draw us closer to the Lord. It can help us deal with things we'd rather ignore. Worship can soften our hearts and make us humbler. Worship can increase our empathy for others in pain. Worship can open hearts. Worship can increase our compassion for others in distress. Worship can open up new ways to experience God's love and comfort. Moreover, our worship can lead us more deeply into the heart of God, who chose to bear our sorrows, and who came in Christ to suffer for us so that we might enjoy the fullness of life.

Do not think that spiritual warfare will not happen because you are worshipping. It will, and it often comes right before unprecedented seasons of God's blessing. If you are experiencing unusual adversity and the timing seems odd, as you are simply trying to impact the kingdom of God, be encouraged that God may be about to bless your efforts significantly. Continue to worship; often, spiritual warfare is the enemy's attempt to steal our happiness about God's actions in our lives. Don't take the bait! Double down on worshipping God and His sovereignty over every situation in your life.

A relationship with God requires open hands and an open heart. While in worship, we must keep our ears open to what He has to say and our minds open to what He asks us to do. We don't need to know the details of the future to fully trust God and obediently take each step He places before us.

God isn't keeping secrets-the bigger picture has been right in front of us the whole time, and this is it: "In all things God works for the good of those who love him, who have been called according to his purpose" (Romans 8:28 NIV). So simple, yet so wonderful. What wondrous love and perfect hope we have because we do not have to carry the future-we need only trust and obey the One who does!

I pray we lean into the freedom found in the arms that carry the heavy weight for us as we let go of the things that weigh us down. He is trustworthy. He is faithful. He is good.

When we worship, our whole focus is on God. It's the best way to block out the enemy's lies because, in a state of worship, we remember who God is, what He brought us out of, and how He can be trusted to do it again.

"We must allow the Word of God to confront us, to disturb our security, to undermine our complacency, and to overthrow our patterns of thought and behavior."

John Stott

His Word is Life

Thank you, God, for allowing me to do good to others daily. Help me to act on those opportunities— even when I don't feel like it. Give me the endurance to serve, the strength to always be kind, and the courage to pray bold prayers on behalf of others. Make me more like You each day. In Jesus' name, Amen.

One of the evils of the human psyche (the soul and the mind) is that we tend to forget the good things and remember the wrong things. Some people can receive a hundred compliments, "You look great. You look beautiful. You are so smart." But if one time they get, “You are a loser," that will stick. We are tempted to remember the bad instead of the good.

You will be happier if your mind is centered on the blessings and mercies you receive. But if you are centered on the injustices you have received, you will soon become bitter.

What is the antidote for forgetfulness? You must preach to yourself frequently—every week, almost every day. Who is Psalm 103 addressed? It is not a prayer; it is not addressed to God. It is not addressed to other people. David is talking to himself. It is as if he is looking at himself in the mirror, saying, "Oh, soul, worship the Lord, praise the Lord, don't forget all His blessings, all His benefits." That is key.

The main issue behind all our problems is that we don't remember the gospel. If any scripture in the Old Testament clearly describes the gospel, it is verses 10 to 12 in Psalm 103, where King David says, “God does not treat us as our sins deserve or repay us according to our iniquities. For as high as the heavens are above the earth, so great is His love for those who fear Him. As far as the east is from the west, He has removed our transgressions from us”.

Let His Light shine through your deeds and actions. Let the Light of Christ be revealed through your words and actions toward each other.

Let His Love flow through your heart. Show others the Love of Christ by showing mercy to those who have done you wrong. Choose to love and forgive freely. When you have the opportunity to do good — choose to do good.

Galatians 6:10 AMPC declares, "So then, as occasion and opportunity open up to us, let us do good [morally] to all people [not only being useful or profitable to them but also doing what is for their spiritual good and advantage]. Be mindful of being a blessing, especially to those of the household of faith [those who belong to God's family with you, the believers]."

Be mindful of doing good to others.

Choose to be a spiritual and natural blessing to others. When it's in your power to do good — extend grace. Extend to them the Lovingkindness of God through your actions. Let your life stand as a living example of God's faithfulness, gentleness, and loving kindness.

"Therefore, whenever we have the opportunity, we should do good to everyone—especially those in the family of faith." Galatians 6:10 NLT

Think about the last time someone was kind to you. Kindness is one of the most potent forces on earth, and serving others can transform someone's life for good.

All of us can do good for someone, and God has gifted us with unique abilities and talents that can be used to serve others in our lives. Whether it's a spiritual gift or a learned skill, you have unique opportunities to show kindness to those in need.

Paul, the writer of the letter to the Galatians, is careful to note that we won't always have the opportunity to do good for others. We cannot know how many days we have left on earth, and we certainly don't know how long certain people will be in our lives. That's why we should use every opportunity to encourage and help others.

Serving and helping others is a form of love. When we take the time to help someone, we allow them to experience the love of Jesus through us. Doing good for someone opens the door to conversations about the love that Jesus has for them.

God, thank you for allowing me to do good to others daily. Help me to act on those opportunities— even when I don't feel like it. Give me the endurance to serve, the strength to always be kind, and the courage to pray bold prayers on behalf of others. Make me more like You each day. In Jesus' name, Amen.

"We're not called to live by human reason. All that matters is obedience to God's Word and His leadership. If God says go, we'll go. If He says stay, we'll stay. When we are in His will, we are in the safest place in the world."

Brother Yun

Obeying God's Call

God, I am honored to be Yours, and I'm grateful that when You created the universe- You thought of me and decided to give me life. Each day, I'm in awe of Your goodness, power, and love for Your people. Thank You for sending Your only Son to the cross so I could have a relationship with You. I love You, Lord. In Jesus' name, Amen.

"Faith motivated Abraham to obey God's call and leave the familiar to discover the territory he was destined to inherit from God. So, he left with only a promise, and Abraham stepped out in faith without knowing where he was going. His eyes of faith were set on the city with unshakable foundations, whose architect and builder are God himself." Hebrews 11:8, 10 TPT

Abraham was motivated by faith, and his eyes were set on Zion, the city of God. In Genesis 12, God spoke to Abraham and promised He would bless Abraham and that all people on earth would be blessed through him. Abraham held onto this promise and followed God into the unknown. Being a human, there's no doubt that there were days when nothing made sense and the promises of God seemed far-fetched and insane. But through all the obstacles and uncertainties, doubts and fears, Abraham was faithful because he had confidence, hope, and assurance that God would do what He said He would do.

The author of the book of Hebrews tells us in chapter 11 that "Faith is confidence in what we hope for and assurance about what we do not see." Faith is confidence. Faith is assurance. But what do we have faith in? Why do we have confirmation? In Hebrews 11:11, we read about Sarah, Abraham's wife, "Sarah's faith embraced God's miracle power to conceive even though she was barren and was past the age of childbearing, for the authority of her faith rested in the One who made the promise, and she tapped into His faithfulness." When the very promise of God doesn't make sense to us, and the world around us is burning down with chaos, we have the choice to grab onto God's miracle power and tap into His faithfulness. We can have confidence because God is faithful. The Bible contains accounts of His dedication to ordinary people, men, and women who trust Him. God is the same yesterday, today, and forever. He is not biased to any specific personality type, gender, age, status, ethnicity, or race. He is faithful, and therefore, we can have confidence.

You might have obstacles or overwhelming situations staring you down, but you can have confidence in God's love, shown through His salvation, because of His faithfulness. You can find rest in His peace and find strength in His joy. He has proven His faithfulness with every generation and made good on every promise from the beginning. The authority of your faith rests in the One who made the promise.

Faith is one of the essential attributes of our entire lives. When we put our faith in Jesus, we have access to eternal life. It is our faith that determines our destiny.

However, faith can be challenging. The writer of Hebrews tells us that trust begins with having confidence in the things we hope for. More than that, it guarantees things we cannot see.

While this sounds contradictory, faith requires us to believe in something outside ourselves. If we could see and measure it, it wouldn't need faith. For instance, we read in Scripture that God created the earth and everything in it. But we weren't there when it happened. It requires faith to believe that.

Jesus says that those who believe in Him will inherit eternal life—but that's a promise yet to come. We have to have faith that Jesus will keep His promise and that one day we will be in heaven with Him.
Faith is the assurance that what God promised will happen. It is the confidence that what Jesus said is true. This is why the heroes in God's Word waited faithfully for God to fulfill His promises toward them. Most of them might not have seen that fulfillment in their lifetime, but they had faith that God would still follow through.

Take some time to consider your faith. Is your faith filled with confident hope? Pray for God to assure you that all His promises will come true. And as you do that, learn from the stories mentioned in Hebrews 11 on what it means to have faith in action.

"We must develop a shepherd's heart and understand the needs of the Lord's sheep. So how do we become the shepherds the Lord needs us to become? As with all questions, we can look to our Savior, Jesus Christ–the Good Shepherd. The Savior's sheep were known and numbered, watched over, and gathered into the fold of God."

Bonnie H. Cordon

Jesus is Our Shepherd.

Loving Father, thank You for this beautiful promise. Thank You, for I am not alone. Give me the grace to seek You with all my heart. Thank You for promising to be my Good Shepherd all the time. Be my Father and guide me beautifully for Your glory. Thank You for Your love. In Jesus' precious name, I pray. Amen.

There are times when I think, how can someone like me succeed? Yet, these thoughts don't devastate me because I know where success comes from. It doesn't matter what it is. It only matters who God is because He is all I need! He is my Jehovah, the Lord my Shepherd. And because the Lord is my Shepherd, I shall not want.

Oh, what a marvelous revelation the Spirit of God gave us as He breathed these words through the pen of David! It's much better to cling to the precepts of God than to maxims or positive thinking because He has magnified His Word above His name (Psalm 138:2).

What does God think about us? Many things—and all of them are precious (Psalm 139:17-18). Yet, His thoughts are based on an honest evaluation of what we are like.

We are like sheep. Over and over again, God refers to us as sheep: "All we like sheep have gone astray" (Isaiah 53:6). "My sheep hear my voice" (John 10:27). "We are...the sheep of His pasture" (Psalm 100:3). "I... will both search my sheep, and seek them out" (Ezekiel 34:11). "Feed my sheep" (John 21:17).

All the positive thoughts in the world can't change the fact that sheep are sheep. Sheep are the dumbest of all animals. They are helpless, timid, and feeble. They require constant attention and meticulous care. Sheep have little means of self-defense.

What makes the difference in sheep is the shepherd.

Even though we do dumb things, are not perfect, and stumble in many ways (James 3:2), we can succeed because the Lord is our Shepherd. God designed us as we are so that we would see our need for Him. In Him, we find all that we need. Thus, we can say with total confidence and conviction, "The Lord is my shepherd; I shall not want" (Psalm 23:1).

As you read through Psalm 23, make a list of all that Jehovah does for His sheep.

The Lord is our water in the desert, and His promises can revive us. No matter what is happening around you, hold on to the promises of our Shepherd; they will give you direction, comfort, and peace. You can trust Him to fulfill all He has told you. Moreover, the Lord has a plan, and you are a part of that plan. Rest in those promises and trust Him for their fulfillment.

On the days when the world gets too much, when - perhaps - you missed the turn-off and had to spend twenty minutes finding your way back, look up and keep your eyes fixed on Him. Ask Him for strength for the day, feel His loving kindness, and enjoy the comfort of Him, who remains the same.

> ***Jesus, the world may change-but You won't. You don't shift. You don't unexpectedly change Your mind or leave us. You give us a consistent example because You are trustworthy and worth pursuing. So please help us to look to You as we go about our daily lives. Help us to follow the example You set. Amen.***

If we are ever to love like our Shepherd, we must push pride to the side and humble our hearts. That's a given. But our Shepherd takes it a step further. He says that if we are to be genuinely approachable and not exclusive, we must do something outrageous. He says we must love our enemies. He says it flat out: "I tell you, love your enemies, bless those who curse you, do good to those who hate you, and pray for those who mistreat you and persecute you."

I don't know about you, but this is an incredibly tough pill to swallow. My nature is inclined to retaliate against those who mistreat me. My impulse is to even the score and then some. I understand loving your neighbor, friends, family, and even strangers. But enemies?

Think again if you believe our Shepherd may have said this flippantly for shock value. He says it more than once and underscores it with examples: "If someone slaps you in the face, stand there and take it. If someone grabs your shirt, gift wrap your best coat and make a present of it. Use the occasion to practice servant life if someone takes unfair advantage of you."

The servant life? This is taking "approachability" to an extreme level. Of course. It's not natural -it's the very opposite of natural. That's why our shepherd also says we can only love in this radical way when we love our "God-created selves." Then he tells us that "God gives his best" ... to everyone, regardless: the good and evil, the friendly and nasty. If all you do is love the lovable, do you expect a bonus? Anybody can do that. If you say hello to those who greet you, do you expect any run-of-the-mill sinner to do that?

I get that. I'm not looking for run-of-the-mill. Like you, I'm looking for the extraordinary. Like you, I aspire to love like my Shepherd.

There was a moment about a year ago when I felt like I was not good enough. I was confused, filled with doubt, and honestly, wondered what life would look like for me in the future. But, as I experience life alongside others, I realize that most of us face moments filled with similar emotions at some point.

How we react to emotions makes the difference in moving through those moments.

Why would we need to trust our Shepherd if life was filled only with mountaintop experiences and no valleys? Most of the time, we limit our thinking to what we can see in the natural when God sees the more incredible picture. He carefully writes our story; He sees what we don't and is faithful.

Looking back on that time a year ago, I now clearly see that God's hand was protecting me, holding me, and ultimately using the feelings of defeat as a part of my story to move me forward.

One character in the Bible who is a great example of trusting God "Every Step of the Way" is Joshua. I love the story in verses one through seven of Joshua chapter four. Joshua has just finished leading his people over the Jordan river and into freedom. It's a huge victory! As a testimony of the miracle they just experienced, Joshua has the people set up twelve stones to memorialize what God did. Those stones would be a reminder so they would never forget!

This is powerful because it's so easy to forget the goodness of our Shepherd in our lives. In our humanness, we tend to quickly jump to the next most remarkable trend, the to-do list, the social media post... you name it.

But what if The Shepherd wants you to rest today and remember what He has done in your life?

How many of us need to set up stones to remember what the Shepherd has done in our lives?

Psalm 77:11, "I shall remember the deeds of the Lord; Surely will remember Your wonders of old."

As long as we let the Word of God be our only armor, we can look confidently into the future.

Dietrich Bonhoeffer

Armor of God

God, thank You for loving me and pursuing a relationship with me. You are everything to me, and I want to seek You first each day. Please be a part of every decision, every thought, every word, and every action I have. My life is Yours. In Jesus' name, Amen.

Uncertainties build up in the mind until every thought is plagued with worry. Panic starts with one concern that quickly leads to a restless feeling, leading to an irrational fear that ultimately leads to extreme anxiety. At this point, panic sets in and takes over. The mind, the emotions, and even the body spins out of control. Worry grapples for power, but ironically, power is precisely what the anxious person loses.

I know about the need for control firsthand. I believed that if things went exactly as I wanted, the entire world would be at peace, and there would be no problems. However, striving for this fantasy made my reality nothing but constant worry, heaviness, sorrow, and desperation. Like the prodigal son, I ran from the Father by trying to control everything myself and ended up in the pigpen.

Perhaps you know what I am talking about. It might not play out the same in your daily life, but you still know what it is like to fight anxiety. Maybe for you, you worry too much. Perhaps, your worry has turned into great fear that has begun to affect your health. Maybe you also suffer from full-blown panic attacks. Wherever you find yourself on this anxiety spectrum, the healing promises of Christ are available to each one of us.

Having God's armor is one thing. Wearing it is another. Putting it on the way a person puts on physical armor requires care and thought. When the enemy has come at you, and he has hit you in every single direction, the number one strategy a believer can employ is to pray.

You're encouraged by the apostle Paul to refrain from making prayer an addendum or an afterthought. You are to make it associated with every aspect of conflict taking place in your life. Whether it's a personal or family conflict, a financial struggle, or being attacked, you might feel like you're not going to make it. That's an invitation to put on the armor of God.

You've got six armor pieces, and you want to wear them because the enemy can physically and circumstantially attack you. What he can't do is defeat you spiritually unless you let him.

So, when Paul tells us to pray without ceasing, he says, "Bring God to bear in everything." Don't have this secular/sacred divide. Make everything holy because when God knows He's a part of everything, He is involved in everything, mainly when our adversary, the devil, is coming against us.

Those six pieces of armor are put on in prayer. You pray in truth. You don the breastplate of righteousness with worship. You're thinking in prayer because sometimes you can't even say it. Finally, you're wielding a sword as you pray through Scripture. You're giving the devil more than he can handle when you pray in this manner. Please put on the armor and watch it repel the evil one.

It is essential to confess what we are struggling with. God can handle your worries, your anger, and your uncertainty. None of it is too big for Him. Make a list of the things you are worried about today. Spend some time handing those worries over to the Lord in prayer.

> ***Thank you, Lord Jesus, for equipping me with everything I need to win my battles this day! I praise you that I am protected today by the armor of God. I now claim your promise that no weapon formed against me shall prosper. In Jesus' mighty name, amen!***

The fruit of the Spirit is not pushing, driving, climbing, grasping, and trampling. Life is more than a climb to the top of the heap.

Richard J. Foster

Two Types of Fruit

Thank you, Lord, for always being willing to hear what's on my heart. I know people in my life need to experience Your love, healing, and guidance, and I want to support them. When I come to You, remind me to also bring the needs of others to You. In Jesus' name, Amen.

Imagine you have two seeds in your hand and can only plant one. One source multiplies, but it produces ugly terrible-tasting fruit. Cultivating the other seed takes time and consistent attention-but. The fruit it has is beautiful and delicious. Which source would you choose to plant, water, and grow?

In Galatians 5, the apostle Paul talks about two fruit our lives can produce: the fruit of the flesh and the fruit of the Spirit. "The flesh" refers to the desires that pull us away from God's Holy Spirit. Those desires produce hate, impatience, bitterness, selfishness, rudeness, chaos, anxiety, and self-indulgence—and God has no association with such things.

But when we commit to Jesus, He gives us His Holy Spirit. The power of the Holy Spirit helps us "crucify" the desires of our flesh and put them to death. And when we crucify those desires, we create room for the Holy Spirit to produce fruit in us that leads to positive life change.

"The fruit of the Spirit is love, joy, peace, forbearance, kindness, goodness, faithfulness, gentleness, and self-control." Galatians 5:22-23 NIV

Our flesh wants to get even, but the Spirit calls us to extend kindness. Our flesh wants to entertain sinful thoughts, but the Spirit calls us to walk in self-control. Our flesh wants to dictate our emotional response. When we commit to Jesus, He gives us His Holy Spirit. The power of the Holy Spirit helps us "crucify" the desires of our flesh and put them to death. And when we crucify those desires, we create room for the Holy Spirit to produce fruit in us that leads to positive life change.

The Fruit of the Spirit reveals that we actively seek God and reject disobedience.

So right now, reflect on your life. What fruit is it producing? Are you experiencing love, joy, peace, patience, and kindness, or are there pockets of bitterness, anger, jealousy, and self-indulgence in your life?

What steps do you need to take to "crucify" beliefs and attitudes pulling you away from God? Let the Holy Spirit show you what you need to remove, and then let Him transform your attitudes, actions, and desires.

God, thank You for giving me a new nature. Because of Jesus, I can know You personally and draw close to You daily. I don't want to take this for granted, so today, I surrender the desires that pull me away from You. Align my will with Your will so I might embrace Your freedom in Jesus' name.

www.ingramcontent.com/pod-product-compliance
Lightning Source LLC
LaVergne TN
LVHW041120150826
845673LV00007B/2131

* 9 7 9 8 3 7 5 6 8 5 8 0 9 *